One

Baptism

Once

by

Colin Buchanan

Honorary Assistant Bishop, Diocese of Rochester
Member of the Church of England Doctrine Commission

GROVE BOOKS LIMITED
Bramcote   Nottingham   NG9 3DS

CONTENTS

THE COVER PICTURE
... is by Peter Ashton

EXTENDED NOTE ON INITIATION SERVICES (from page 3 opposite)

This particular booklet was a commentary on GS 225, the 1975 report by the Liturgical Commission which contained a draft service of infant baptism only. The print-run was a short one, as it was clear that General Synod would revise the service before authorization. Thus the commentary too would have had to be revised for a second edition. In the event, as was easy to foresee, Synod could not go ahead with the text at all, as they were still handling the debate on principles of initiation. By the time that this was over, the Liturgical Commission was nearly ready to produce a whole set of draft services for initiation—including adult and household baptism, confirmation, and the services of Thanksgiving for the Birth of a Child and for Adoption. These were published as GS 343 on 18 August 1977, and were given 'General Consideration' in November 1977. They were duly revised and then authorized in 1978 and published in 1979. Booklet no. 65, *Liturgy for Initiation: The Series 3 Services* is a commentary on them. Finally they were incorporated into the Alternative Service Book 1980.

First Edition October 1978

Second Edition September 1983

Third Edition (by Grove Books Limited) November 1989

ISSN 0305-3067

ISBN 1 85174 126 7

INTRODUCTION TO THIRD EDITION

Since the early 1970s I have written several times in this series on Christian initiation—*Baptismal Discipline* (no. 3, 1972), *A Case for Infant Baptism* (no. 20, 1973), *Infant Baptism under Cross-Examination* (jointly with David Pawson, no. 24, 1974), *The Liturgy for Infant Baptism (Series 3)* (no. 37, 1975),[1] the first edition of this Booklet, *One Baptism Once* (no. 61, 1978), *Liturgy for Initiation: The Series 3 Services* (no. 65, 1979), *Adult Baptisms* (no. 91, 1985), and *Policies for Infant Baptism* (no. 98, a re-write of no. 3, 1987). I have also written *Anglican Confirmation* (Liturgical Study, no. 48, 1986), and contributions to journals and symposia. Most of the titles are (in a first or later edition) currently still in print, and a continuing demand has led to this third edition of no. 61.

It is not only whether there is a case for *infant* baptism that we have to consider, but also whether there is a sufficient case for baptism itself. it is not only whether or not to advise parents to have their children baptized that we have to consider, but also what to say to those seeking 'rebaptism'.[2] I conceive it to be needed for pastoral reasons, and it is with the pastor's responsibilities in sight that I have written.

The intention of the booklet is that everything in it should be demonstrable from scripture. But that does not mean that we have to ignore the lessons of history. It is inevitable that we should have had our attitudes formed by the various pressures of Christian history, either directly or by our conscious reaction against them. It is therefore as well if we recognize these pressures, and scrutinize them coolly to see how valid they have been.

This inevitability of the forces of history is particularly important in relation to baptism, as in England we move into the last phase of the transition from being part of 'Christendom' to being a genuinely pluralist society, and thus a country in need of Christian mission. This, I take it, has its parallels with the Roman Empire in which the Christian mission first came to birth, and thus we may now try the more successfully to administer baptism in the 'New Testament way'. But we cannot escape history even so, and there are constant reminders that we are only *beginning* the last phase of the transition from 'Christendom', and we do not know how long that phase will prove to be.

In earlier booklets I mentioned my hope, treasured now for over two decades, that I might one day be able to write a weighty hardback on baptism. That day is still as far off as ever. Against that distant hope this booklet must be seen as yet another stopgap. But if it does stop a gap, then it will have been well worth it.

Since the first edition was published, I have disciovered a growng need for a renewal of baptismal vows in water, and I add an appendix on this. I have also become president of the Movement for the Reform of Infant Baptism (MORIB), a pressure group to assist the transition mentioned above.

Colin Buchanan   31 October 1989

[1] See extended note on Contents page opposite re no 37.

[2] 'Rebaptism' is of course an impossible concept. This is discussed at some length on pages 18 to 20 below.

1. WHAT IS A BAPTISM?

Much of current writing on baptism would have been rendered unnecessary if the New Testament writers had taken time off from solving the other problems of the church, whether doctrinal or moral, and had instead answered the question 'What is Baptism?'. As they failed in this apparently obvious duty, the rest of us have been left to read between the lines of the New Testament and infer from that what the answer to the question would have been. What is perfectly clear is that the New Testament writers ignored the question not because they could not answer it, but because to them the answer was so blindingly obvious as to need no discussion. Their references to baptism are therefore almost invariably allusive and passing.

If we come at this a different way, then the summary assertions with which I began the *Case* in booklet no. 20 may be repeated to establish the present agenda:

'Baptism is one and common to all Christians. This is surely the implication of Eph. 4.4—"One Lord, one faith, one baptism". There can no more be a denominational baptism than a denominational Christ (which is exactly the thrust of 1 Cor. 1 also). Baptism cannot be simply a subjective experience—it must demand recognition by the church through the world.

'Baptism is once and for all and for life. Because it initiates (into the church, into salvation, into Christ, into the new life) it cannot be repeated. A person is either baptized or unbaptized. Once baptized he cannot become unbaptized again.

'It follows that there must be a good rule-of-thumb definition as to what is to rank as a baptism.'[1]

I think the logic of this stands. *If* baptism is once for all for life, *then* we must know when it has been administered and when it has not. And this in turn brings us to the question of definition.

The problem of efficacy
In the New Testament baptism is (usually) treated as effecting what it signifies. This has never been a problem to the 'Catholic' parts of the Christian church, as they have been content to assert that baptism *is* invariably efficacious[2] and *does* effect what it signifies.[3] The problem this form of exegesis sets up is that it seems to involve asserting some or all of the following highly doubtful sayings:

1 Booklet no. 20, p.7.
2 To be fair to the 'Catholic 'standpoint, it should be pointed out that they have not traditionally held that *adult* baptism is invariably efficacious. The adult can place an *'obex'* (a barrier) in the path of grace, through impenitence or hypocrisy, and thus not receive the grace. But this is not true of an infant, who has no capacity to erect an *obex,* and thus does invariably receive the grace. Even so, that statement does not necessarily imply that the grace will be seen in his life—unless he chooses to 'co-operate' with grace, it will remain unfruitful. (This, to some minds, is to nullify 'grace' by a fatal qualification . . .).
3 Note the language of apparent efficacy in Mt. 28.19, John 3.5, Acts 2.38, Acts 22.16, Rom. 6.3-4, 1 Cor. 12.13, Gal. 3.27, Col. 2.12, 1 Pet. 3.21 and many other places.

1. Regeneration (which all agree is signified in baptism) may be effected in a person *without there being any visible evidence in his or her life.* (But what then of Nicodemus' words, in a passage about rebirth by water and the Spirit, that 'you hear the sound of it'—i.e., presumably, that the wind/Spirit has clear effects in a man's life, even though its origin and destination are mysterious to us (John 3.8) ?)
2. Baptism brings justification unconditionally. (But if faith brings justification, then logically baptism *tout simple* does not—and *vice versa*—as faith and baptism are not the same thing.)
3. Baptism grafts persons into the church, the living body of Christ. (But this seems impossible unless there is life in the persons themselves . . .)

Because this type of assertion is unwelcome to the evangelical, he has tended to take refuge in one or more of the following exegetical expedients:

1. He may simply *not want to know* that scripture speaks of baptism in terms of efficacy.
2. He may try to expound the relevant passages by saying that they presuppose the inward gift, and that true baptism (which is the only efficacious kind) involves that pre-supposition.
3. He may go further and deny that references to baptism are references to the administration of water at all, and insist that they simply refer to the inward experience of being 'flooded' with the Holy Spirit.
4. He may go not quite so far, but may merely deny that these references to baptism can refer to infant baptism. From this standpoint, an adult baptism may be a passing from death to life, or a being united with Christ in his death and resurrection, but an infant baptism cannot be.
5. Any or all of the positions above are still likely to drive him to a very 'low' view of water-baptism—so that it becomes a mere token of a conversion actually effected at some other time (whether before or after the baptism), and in many cases has to be re-expounded as a 'witness' to a conversion effected earlier—i.e. it is a point of public confession of Christ.

It is probable in the Church of England that in the last 150 years, and certainly since the time of the Gorham controversy[1], we have been seeing

[1] George Cornelius Gorham, an incumbent in Cornwall, was subjected to a cross-examination about his views on baptism by his diocesan bishop, Dr. Henry Philpotts of Exeter, when he was nominated by the Lord Chancellor for another living in the diocese. The initial examination by the bishop occupied eight whole days in December 1847 and March 1848. The bishop then refused to institute Gorham, on the grounds that his view that not all infants are necessarily and invariably regenerated in baptism was heretical and contrary to the doctrine of the creeds, the Prayer Book and the Articles of Religion. Gorham then had to ask the Provincial Court of Canterbury—the Court of Arches—for an injunction requiring Philpotts to institute him. The bishop was the defendant in this hearing—but it was Gorham's doctrine which was on trial. The Court of Arches found for the bishop in August 1849. Gorham then appealed to what was then the final court of appeal in ecclesiastical cases, the Judicial Committee of the Privy Council. Here he was much helped by the work of William Goode, whose *magnum opus* on this subject, *The Effects of Infant Baptism,* was first published in 1849. This work showed that Gorham stood

[continued on page 6 overleaf]

tne sharp-edged forms of 'catholic' and 'evangelical' beliefs about the efficacy of baptism polarizing further and further from each other.[1] Yet the former does not do justice to the biblical teaching about the experience of rebirth and the coming of the Spirit, and the latter does not do justice to the biblical teaching about the efficacy of baptism.

It is not my intention here to attempt a full resolution of these problems of efficacy, as my main aim is to explore the effect of the 'low' view on the *practice* of baptism. But I set out some lines of approach to a resolution:

1. We must hold onto biblical teaching—whether it refers to rebirth or to the efficacy of baptism—*as a totality*. We cannot solve our problems by the rationalistic building of a 'system' which is consistent and logical and based upon certain truths of scripture, if the price of such tidiness is the dropping of other parts of scripture altogether.

2. Some of our problems have arisen, in the case of adult baptisms, by the churches' fondness for delaying baptism till well after conversion so that the two events are clearly separated. Then if the one is efficacious, the other is not. And a rationale still has to be found for baptism, so it becomes a public testimony. In the scriptures, the invariable practice of the New Testament Church was to baptize at the moment of conversion, as the *means* of conversion. So the archetypes of baptism present a different rationale from the latter day constructions.[2]

3. Other problems have arisen, in the case of infant baptism, through the practice of 'indiscriminate' baptism, which has meant that baptism has lost all relationship to the beginning of the Christian life, for many

---

[1] As I sent this edition to press the Doctrine Commission has completed a book on the Holy Spirit in which *this* polarization proved the hardest to handle.

[2] I have set out the case for this New Testament approach to adult baptism in booklet no. 20 on pp.15-16. It reads differently from a Baptist rationale.

---

continued from page 5]

in live succession to the English reformers and a great company of Anglican divines since—and that Philpotts' doctrine had only achieved any mainstream significance in the Church of England since 1815! The Judicial Committee duly reversed the Court of Arches' judgment and found for Gorham in March 1850. The finding was that Gorham's doctrine, as stated below in the words of the judgment, was not contrary or repugnant to the doctrine of the Church of England. The position was stated as follows:

'That Baptism is a Sacrament generally necessary to salvation, but that the grace of regeneration does not so necessarily accompany the act of Baptism that regeneration invariably takes place in Baptism; that the grace may be granted before, in, or after Baptism; that Baptism is an effectual sign of grace, by which God works invisibly in us, but only in such as worthily receive it— in them alone it has a wholesome effect; and that without reference to the qualifications of the recipient, it is not in itself an effectual sign of grace. That infants baptized, and dying before actual sin, are certainly saved; but that in no case is regeneration unconditional.' (J. C. S. Nias *Gorham and the Bishop of Exeter* (S.P.C.K., 1951) p.98).

This finding, whilst it might not meet the exact approval of all evangelicals, safeguarded evangelicals in their position in the Church of England, and antagonized anglo-catholics. Had Philpotts been upheld, there would have been no place for evangelicals, and the tenseness of the controversy reflected that awareness.

of the candidates are *not actually beginning anything* (except in the most dry and formal sense). Thus again there is no clear connection in anyone's mind between baptism and actually beginning.

4. Further problems have arisen through the fondness (of all parties in the discussion of baptismal efficacy) for talking in *individualistic* terms. The discussion is about what *this* event has (or has not) done for *this* individual. But in fact baptism is also an *ecclesial* event, with strong implications for the church. Whatever else it does, it indubitably provides new members for the church. But that is simply for the church visible, you answer. True, it is, but then, at root, our problem may well be not a 'low' view of baptism, but a 'low' view of the visible church. Perhaps the argument ought to start there. Certainly the doctrine of the church as visible has been a notorious blindspot amongst evangelicals.

5. The efficacy in scripture is not absolutely invariable. In Acts 8.4 the baptisms were not attended by the gift of the Spirit. In 1 Cor. 10.1-6 Paul warns the readers '... Our fathers were all baptized [in the manner of a type[1], by going through the Red Sea] ... nevertheless with most of them God was not pleased ... these things are warnings for us ...' Here there seems to be a very clear warning that being baptized can, of itself, leave a man still far from God—and the New Testament Churches bear ample witness to the mixed multitude which had come through the waters of baptism and still had no experience of the risen life in Christ.

6. So how then should we return to the language of efficacy which remains the standard usage of the New Testament? Surely, by treating it as true (for it is as much part of the biblical revelation as any other teaching found by frequent allusion in the New Testament), but as *not unconditionally* true.[2] What this means in practical terms is that the baptized are *prima facie* entitled to be treated as believers—and paradoxically, that people turn out as they are treated. This in turn has implications for our preaching and teaching about baptism—it should be handled positively and constructively, and not be denounced as a hindrance which has inoculated people against catching the real infectious Christianity.[3]

The effect of 'evangelical' thinking

For the moment, we return to the 'evangelical' cartoon description on page 5 above. Our task is to undermine the effects of this thinking upon evangelical practice. We discern three important kinds of effect.

1. The definition includes the efficacy, which defeats its purpose

If the scriptures can only be understood by our insisting that baptism is only baptism when it includes the experience of the inward gift of

---

[1] Verse 11 says 'These things happened to them as a type [Greek *tupikos*, "typ-ically"]'.

[2] As noted above (footnote 2 on p.4 above) *no-one* holds that the language is unconditionally true of adult candidates. In the Gorham case (footnote 1 on p.5 above) Gorham held that there was at this point a deeper unity between infant and adult baptism than his opponents would concede.

[3] This point is handled on pp.21-22 below. There are rare exceptions in the New Testament (of which the 1 Cor. 10 passage is most obvious one), where the apostle can in effect say 'You were baptized ... but it has done many of you no good'.

7

rebirth, then a whole host of further implications follows.[1] In the first instance, we cannot know for certain when a baptism *is* a baptism. We may administer the water, but God alone knows the heart, and he alone therefore knows whether a man was 'truly' baptized or not. In the second instance, therefore, we cannot keep baptismal registers, we cannot issue baptismal certificates, we cannot appeal in our preaching to the fact of being baptized persons[2]—for we do not know whether or not baptism in the true sense has ever actually occurred, even though water may have been thrown around at some point! In the third instance, therefore, we deliver many people, especially those who were watered as infants, but also those who were submerged in their teens, into thinking that because they cannot reckon that they had at the point of watering the true inward gift of the Spirit, they therefore cannot have been baptized when they were watered, and they ought now to seek real baptism. Although there *is* a difference between efficacy and inefficacy, it is not always open to inspection at a moment's notice, it may be for a long time known to God alone, and we dare not suspend the *definition* of baptism upon it.

2. Baptism as a witness may seem otiose and be omitted

Any view which downgrades the importance of the outward rite of administering water runs the severe risk of making that rite unnecessary. There is a strong tendency amongst many evangelical Christians to use baptism as an individual 'witness' to conversion (with some dramatic symbolism added). This in turn means that church membership can be separated from baptism, so that the unbaptized can be members, can be communicant, and can even be church officers and ministers. And, if the right opportunity for the 'witness' is lost, then as the months and years go by it becomes more and more irrelevant (or even embarrassing) to wish to go through this witnessing rite. As undergoing baptism is seen as an individual response to a particular inner call by Christ to a particular step of individual discipleship, the corollary is that many will never feel that particular call at all, and will thus never seek baptism. This stands over against a necessity for baptism according to the New Testament.[3]

3. Baptism becomes valued solely or largely as an experience

The somewhat subjective approach to the sacrament which the two categories of effect set out above reflect reaches its logical conclusion when baptism is measured by the candidate according to how he or she *felt*. Was God at work in him? Was the plunging memorable?

[1] In booklet no. 20 on p.28 I quote Dunn's 'epigrammatic' summary that 'Baptism demands faith for its validity' *(Baptism in the Spirit* (S.C.M., 1970) p.228). This is a scholar's statement of the very principle I am trying here to oppose.

[2] At best we would keep baptismal registers in pencil and issue certificates in invisible ink. It is this point which inspired the (orthodox!) cover-picture. But we would preach telling those who had been watered that they had *not* thereby been baptized —and would thus in time be offering them 'true' baptism if they would only repent.

[3] Necessity? Well, in Matt. 28.19, the 'baptizing' is *virtually* causal (i.e. it means *'by* baptizing'), and not merely coincidental; in John 3 'water' is connected with the necessity of the new birth; in Acts 2 baptism is virtually instrumental (in the way it is cited) in bringing the gift of the Spirit; in Romans 6 it is instrumental in bringing union with Christ; in Gal. 3.27 it is virtually instrumental in our 'putting on Christ'; and so one could go on.

Was the occasion one where the presence of God was sensed by those present? It is sufficient for the moment to note this stance without commenting on it.

These effects cut baptism loose from the doctrine of the church, and make it a will o' the wisp which anyone can chase at will, anyone can ignore if desired, and the one-eyed can chase as a life's pre-occupation.

It is true that these complaints sound as though they are pitched against Baptists.[1] To an extent they are. Not all Baptists fall deeply into these ways of thinking, and perhaps very few go to the logical limits of their position. But the *tendency* of Baptist thinking is in this direction, and these effects live on—in tension with the New Testament patterns—in very many Baptists. It is certainly true that if these ways of thought prevail, then there is no rationale left for infant baptism *as* baptism. It will not conform to any of the criteria which emerge. To that extent these attitudes lead Christians to becoming Baptists. But it would be wrong to sweep all rejecters of infant baptism into the same mould of thinking, and in respect of Baptists I simply want to say 'If the cap fits, please wear it—if not, no-one will insist it does.'

But my main concern is with the incipient growth of this thinking amongst Anglicans, who have to have a rationale for infant baptism, but yet seem to want to pull out the rug from under it. No doubt there are laudable concerns for the reality and importance of Christian experience. These are figuring very strongly at the present time. They are central biblical issues. But stressing them does not justify distorting baptism into an unbiblical shape. All scripture must be held in balance.

Towards a definition

The polarized pictures set out over against each other above point up the need for us to distinguish between 'efficacy' and 'validity'. To use the word 'validity' may sound like a retreat to the Middle Ages and the world of scholastic theology.[2] But it is not really so. If baptism is once and for all and for life, then it is crucially important to the church to know who has received it, and who has not, and it is vital to the individual to know whether he has been baptized or not.

Anyone who says 'Well, I *was* baptized as a baby, but who can call *that* "baptism"?' is inevitably invoking the category of validity. Was an event a baptism, or was it not? That is the sum of the issue involved in 'validity'.[3] This category of 'validity' cannot be discarded in respect of a once-for-all rite, and if the word 'validity' is banned, then some other word will have to be employed to serve exactly the same role as 'validity'. In other words, we need a *definition* which will tell us when a baptism was a baptism—i.e.

[1] I use 'Baptists' here in the way defined in booklet no. 20, p.3—that is to include any who deny that an infant baptism is a baptism at all. They may or may not be members of the Baptist denomination. The same terminology (but without the capital 'B') is used by Bridge and Phypers in *The Waters that Divide* (IVP, 1977).

[2] We do not of course have to delve into the realm of the 'indelible character'—which it was supposed was an impress on a man's soul! 'Validity' can shake clear of those encumbrances.

[3] It will be noted that not only Roman Catholics and traditionalists are committed to this word. In footnote 1 on p.8 above I have quoted J. D. G. Dunn, who was using it presumably in the same sense (though with very different criteria of validity!).

when it was 'valid'—and, as we have seen, it will be perilous to suspend that definition upon subjective considerations.

This last point may be gently reinforced from the scriptures. In the two instances of 'inefficacy' cited on page 7 above, there is no question that the baptisms were valid. In Acts 8, when Philip has brought the Samaritans to baptism, we are told (verse 16) 'For he [the Holy Spirit] had not yet fallen upon any of them, but they had merely been baptized into the name of the Lord Jesus.' So here, although the distinctive Christian experience was missing, the Samaritans have beyond all doubt been baptized (and the case can be further reinforced by citing Simon Magus). The apostles who come down from Jerusalem do not say 'Ah, these folk did not receive the Spirit when Philip poured water on them, so that was not a true baptism'. Rather they said 'They have received baptism, and therefore we must not attempt to baptize them as though they had not —rather we have to minister the inner gift of the Holy Spirit by prayer and laying on of hands'.

The same is true of the 1 Corinthians 10 episode also mentioned on page 7 above. The baptism of the Israelites in the Red Sea was in many cases inefficacious in the sense of giving them a right relationship with God. The implication is that the same may be true of the baptism of the Corinthians. Paul does *not* say 'All our fathers went through the waters of the Red Sea but only some were baptized.'[1] If he had done, the reference to the Corinthians would work out similarly, 'And all of you have been through the waters, but not all have been baptized and have the Holy Spirit'. He allows that baptism may be inefficacious (in terms of the individual's relationship with God), but that does not mean it is not baptism. Its validity is wholly separable from its efficacy.

Thus we come to the question of definition. We are finding that subjective matters cannot be introduced into the definition. To decide whether an event was or was not a baptism we shall have to have reference to external criteria alone. For the moment we need not insist on a uniformity of mode or formula, though these are handled briefly in the Appendixes.[2] We are therefore approaching a definition as follows:

'Baptism is the administration of water on a person, with sufficient wording to establish that Christian baptism is intended.'[3]

At first sight this minimal definition may look circular. If that is a baptism which says it is, how can the circle be broken? The answer to this is that although it cannot be broken, it can be enlarged—and arguing in a circle has always been viewed as more and more acceptable the larger the circle is. The circle is enlarged very greatly by a statement as to what Christianity is (so that we know it is *Christian* baptism in view). That statement is itself infinitely enlargeable. Then, within that Christian circle, the statement will be further enlarged by expositions of the meaning (and thus the unrepeatability) of baptism. But these background statements must be taken for granted when approaching a definition which will indicate whether a certain person has been baptized or not. The only exceptions are where deviant sects have administered a rite called baptism. Unitarian

1 See booklet no. 20. p.29, footnote 1.
2 See p.24 below.
3 Compare my definition in booklet no. 20, p.29: '. . . baptism is true Christian baptism where the administration of water is performed with some expression of its uniting to Christ or to the Trinity, in an orthodox Christian context.'

baptism *cannot* be Christian baptism. Nor can Mormon or Jehovah's Witnesses baptism. So, although we need objective criteria to establish the validity of particular baptisms, it is insufficient to insist, for example, that the phrase 'in the name of the Father and of the Son and of the Holy Spirit' or 'into the Lord Jesus' should have been used. A baptism may be a baptism without these.[1] Or, if it is in a heretical context, it may not be a baptism when one of these formulae is used. On the other hand, the phrase *'that Christian baptism is intended'* in the definition is looking towards the objective *context* of the administration, and is *not* concerned with the beliefs, hopes or morals of the particular administrant who applies the water. These are not accessible, even if they were relevant. In the mercy of God, he has not insisted on our obtaining the unobtainable in order to establish the validity of a baptism.

The main thrust of these objective criteria is to take the weight off the individual qualifications, *as a basis of definition.* The only place where it would be relevant to ask about individual subjective feelings would be where the candidate was actually unwilling, and was in some way being coerced against his conscience. But even then, unpleasant though the conclusion may be, the church would be wise to accept the consequences that this *was* a baptism, albeit under totally regrettable circumstances, rather than allow the possibility of *post factum* claims that a baptism was not a baptism on the grounds of unwillingness.

Leaving aside the whole matter of infants (who are presumably neither noticeably willing nor noticeably unwilling), there are many teenagers (in all denominations) who go through baptism under various sorts of parental or peer-group pressure. It would be easy later to call this 'coercion' and to try to invalidate the baptism retrospectively. There are degrees and degrees of coercion and unwillingness, and it is safer, even in the most unpleasant or unsavoury cases of it, not to allow even this subjective criterion to invalidate the baptism.

But the point of looking for the one, just arguable, loophole in the objective pattern of definition, is to emphasize the more weightily that there are no other loopholes. The criteria by which validity is tested are objective—the water and the liturgical (verbal) context. This in no way excuses the church from the task of sifting candidates and accepting only the right ones, if possible. It is a mere assertion that a certain event *was* a baptism, even if it is later arguable that the church ought not to have administered it when it did to that particular candidate. The fact that it should not have been administered is no more an argument that it was therefore not a baptism than the fact that two people ought not to have married each other is an argument that therefore they did not. It does not matter to the question as to whether a baptism *was* a baptism or not whether the candidate was old or young, male or female, knowledgeable or ignorant, buoyed up or depressed, or even believing or unbelieving—these grounds may well affect the *suitability* of that particular baptism, but they do not touch its *validity*.

[1] As shown on p.24 below, the rite described in the *Apostolic Tradition* of Hippolytus in the early third century involved an interrogation of candidates standing in the water. They said 'I believe' to the three questions about the creed, and were then watered without further formula by the minister of baptism. This *was* baptism into the Father the Son and the Holy Spirit.

2 WHY BE BAPTIZED?

We have seen above that there is a temptation for those who reckon they know Christ by faith, to draw the conclusion from this that they therefore have no need of an external ceremony like baptism. This temptation may be assisted by the invoking of certain passages of scripture which seem to make baptism unnecessary. These are:

1. The dying thief (Luke 23.42-3). It is obvious that this man was accepted by God without baptism, and it is natural to refer to him as indicating the non-necessity of it.
2. Cornelius (Acts 10.44-48). The first Gentile to be converted received the Spirit first, and only received baptism afterwards. It is obvious that he did not *need* baptism for salvation.
3. The argument from justification through faith (as, e.g., in Rom. 3.21-26 or Gal. 3.21-26). The essence of this argument is basic to the whole approach.
4. The argument from the 'non-efficacious' instances of baptism (Acts 8 and 1 Cor. 10). These further assist the line of reasoning which says baptism is unnecessary—after all, it did not do these particular recipients any good!

Against these lines of reasoning it must be asserted that the whole thrust of the New Testament (admittedly drawn from allusive references) teaches the exact opposite—that baptism is mandatory for all the people of God. And, indeed, the passages cited above can then be seen to fit into the standard pattern, rather than to be foundation evidence for a different pattern.

What then is the necessity for baptism? If we grant that it is not absolutely essential for salvation, in the sense that the unbaptized are *ipso facto* lost, even if they have faith in Christ, then what degree of necessity does it have? This can be best understood by looking at several convergent lines of answers.

1. Baptism is a constituent part of the gospel

On the day of Pentecost, the gospel message was 'Repent and be baptized . . . and you will receive the gift of the Spirit' (Acts 2.38). To receive the word was to be baptized (Acts 2.41). Similarly, when the Samaritans 'believed Philip' (Acts 8.12)—though, as we have seen, they did not then receive the Spirit—they submitted to baptism. When Philip preached the gospel of Jesus to the Ethiopian eunuch (Acts 8.35) the response to it was 'Here is water! What is to hinder my being baptized?'. When Saul was converted, the completion of that conversion was baptism (Acts 9.18, 22.16). There are conversions in Acts which do not record baptism (just as there are conversions which do not record repentance). But there are ample records of conversions which do include baptism for us to see that submission to the gospel included submission to baptism—or alternatively that submission to baptism was reckoned to be submission to the gospel.

2. Baptism is universally practised among Christians

By this I do not mean that all believers everywhere have always practised baptism (though in fact the exceptions to this are very very few), but rather that in the New Testament the practice is universally taken for granted. That is to say that Paul, when writing to any of the Churches, can appeal to the fact that they are all baptized people as the fulcrum on which he can then place the lever of the word. There are many instances, but 1 Corinthians 1 provides as good an example as any.[1] Here Paul puts up the rhetorical questions 'Is Christ divided? Was Paul crucified for you? Or were you baptized into the name of Paul?' (1 Cor. 1.12). The clear inference behind these questions is that there is one undivided Christ, that that Christ was crucified for them, and that they had all been baptized into his name

We may put this 'taking for granted' the other way round. It is fair to say that the New Testament knows nothing of the unbaptized Christian. As I have pointed out at greater length elsewhere[2], there was no catechumenate, no probationary period, no time of instruction prior to baptism in the New Testament. The longest gap between 'conversion' and baptism is the three days of Saul (Acts 9.9)—and even then it may be more appropriate to count his conversion from the same time as his baptism, for he was in darkness until then. In all other cases baptism and conversion are so closely entwined that the beginning of the Christian life can be traced equally easily to the inward or the outward.

The New Testament church was a universal body, manifested in local fellowships, also called churches. There was no individualistic Christianity independently of membership of the church. To respond to the gospel was to respond to an embodied message of love. The only credible response was to join the fellowship embodying the message. Conversion was conversion *into the community.* In the words of the Acts, newcomers were *both* 'added to their number' (Acts 2.47) *and* 'added to the Lord' (Acts 5.14). But the only way to join the community was by baptism into Christ—the 'saints' (or holy people) were the baptized ones. The unbaptized were still, from the point of view of the church, mere enquirers. To be reckoned as converted they still would have to be baptized. If they hung back from baptism, it was not because they wanted to be Christians without baptism (for the whole idea would have been incomprehensible to them). It was only that they were still wavering, and were unready for the total response to the gospel which baptism implied.

3. Baptism identifies people as Christian
We have seen that all believers in the New Testament days received baptism at conversion. We have seen that to receive baptism was to be treated as a believer and to be incorporated into the church. The corollary of all this is that the church offered no fellowship to the unbaptized whilst they were unbaptized. They were still outside the community. We cannot know what Peter would have said on the day of Pentecost if his hearers had replied to 'Repent and be baptized . . . and you will receive the gift of the Holy Spirit' by saying 'We will repent, and we do want the gift of the Spirit. But we will not be

---

[1] Others include Rom. 6.2-7, 1 Cor. 12.13, Gal. 3.27, Eph. 4.5, Col. 2.11-12, etc.
[2] Booklet no. 20, pp.15-16.

baptized.' But it is a fair guess, in the light of the general trend of the New Testament, that he would have said 'God alone knows your hearts, but you have neither part nor lot with us till you receive *all* that I bring you of the gospel. You are not to pick and choose what you will have and what you will not. Without baptism we cannot recognize you as repenting or believing. Repent truly therefore—and repent in the waters of baptism.' The Christian church has no warrant or reason for treating the unbaptized as believers, or extending any form of Christian fellowship to them. It has only one message for them, and it is this: 'Here is water—repent and be baptized'.

In the light of these convergent lines of reasoning, we can return to see whether the original arguments (that baptism is strictly speaking unnecessary) have any force. On inspection, we find that, far from being normative and mainstream, they are perverse and untenable as grounds for making baptism a purely optional rite. We review the four headings again:

1. *The dying thief.* We recall that this man was accepted by God *both* before the beginning of ordered church life on the day of Pentecost, *and* in the last moments of his earthly life. There can therefore be nothing normative here for the normal church life of the living after the day of Pentecost.

2. *Cornelius.* This man may well have needed to exhibit the gift of the Spirit before baptism, as Peter needed some unusually strong warrant before he would see baptism as appropriate.[1] But the important question to us is 'What did Peter then do?' And the answer is that he looked round for the water as quickly as possible. In effect he had (to use the words set out above) only one message for the household of Cornelius when this happened 'Here is water—get baptized quickly.' This confirms our reasoning that there is only one thing the church can say to the unbaptized who profess faith.

3. *The argument from justification through faith.* This is a rationalistic dichotomizing of faith and baptism.[2] In fact, both Romans and

---

[1] Note his horror-struck recoiling from the whole idea of receiving Gentiles into fellowship (Acts 10.9-16). It is arguable that the particular instances of glossolalia in Acts announce steps forward into new spheres for the gospel—in Acts 2 heralding the mission to Jerusalem and all Judaea, in Acts 8 to Samaria, and in Acts 10 to the Gentiles (and in Acts 19 catching up on the curious sect of remote followers of John the Baptist).

[2] Of course Paul says in 1 Cor. 1. 'Christ sent me not to baptize, but to preach the gospel'. But this must not be misunderstood. He cannot be saying 'I have a gospel to preach and baptism is a distraction from it or an excrescence upon it.' He must rather be saying 'My personal task in the gospel was the preaching, not the administering of the baptisms.' This is in line with his need to deny solely that he had performed the baptisms (which therefore could not be a pretext for the formation of a 'Paul-party'). It is also in line with the general apostolic practice of assigning responsibility for conducting baptisms to their assistants or minions—cf. Acts 10.48 'He commanded that they should be baptized'. Indeed the *active* of 'baptize' is only used in Acts 8.38 (where there was only one person who could baptize present anyway—and he a deacon!), in Matt. 28, 19-20, and in this 1 Cor. 1 passage, in respect of Christian converts. All other uses are passive.

14

Galatians (and most of the other letters) *interchange* faith and baptism without warning. Thus in Romans 6 Paul writes:

> 'Shall we continue in sin that grace may abound? God forbid. How shall we who have died to sin still live in it? Or are you unaware that those of us who were baptized into Christ were baptized into his death? . . .'

But for the purposes of his argument he could just as well have written:

> '. . . Or are you unaware that those of us who have believed in Christ have been united with him in his death? . . .'

The argument that 'death to sin' comes through baptism is simply a variant version of the argument that justification comes through faith!

The interchange is even more obvious in Galatians 3. In Galatians 3.26 Paul writes (in the context of asserting justification through faith):

> 'For you are all sons of God through faith in Christ Jesus.'

For the purposes of this argument, he might well have gone on to say in verse 27:

> 'For as many of you as have believed in Christ have put on Christ.'

But in fact he quite unselfconsciously continues (as though it were an exact logical equivalent):

> 'For as many of you have been baptized into Christ have put on Christ.'

We thus have to conclude that, however much a tightly consistent theory of justification through faith alone might appear to preclude the possibility of an outward sacramental component in that justification, in fact any argument of this sort from Paul's actual writings will quickly stumble and fall flat. His insistent recourse to the quite 'unnecessary' mention of baptism shows that the argument would have no force with him. Be his logic consistent or inconsistent, he smoothly interchanges his terms, from faith to baptism and back again, and gives no opportunity for the reliance on faith to preclude the necessity of baptism.

4. *The argument from the 'non-efficacious' instances of baptism.* This argument proves too much. For the fact of the matter is that (in Samaria, for instance) it was deemed right to give baptism even when apparently the 'converts' were not receiving the Spirit thereby—and in the case of Simon Magus the 'convert' was clearly undoubtedly hypocritical. And yet they *were* baptized. We might rather conclude from these occasional instances that, even where there was some doubt about the reality of 'conversion', yet the apostolic church administered baptism to those who merely professed faith. Certainly the mixed character of the New Testament churches would bear this out. Far from the random 'non-efficacy' of baptism being an argument for dispensing with it, the evidence which is being adduced about it is itself grounded upon a universal consensus by the early church that baptism would be administered even in cases where doubt about the inward gift existed.

We conclude from this that, whether it was received genuinely or hypo-critically, baptism was universally administered, and it admitted its recipi-ents into the universal church of Christ.[1] All were bound together by 'One Lord, one faith, one baptism' (Eph. 4.5)—or, as it might be better translated, 'One Lord in common, one faith in common, one baptism in common.' Because the sacramental initiation was 'once for all for life', it was no domestic or local or ephemeral ceremony. The man who received it remained a baptized person wherever he went for the rest of his life. Baptism marked him in a way comparable to the way Jewish circumcision marked him—the initiatory sign was not just a fleeting experience, but an identification of a man's community membership for the rest of his life.

The question is: do we see baptism in the same way as the New Testament church did?

---

[1] Because baptism 'admits', the unbaptized are *ipso facto* unadmitted. This in turn means that the unbaptized are not admissible to communion—at the very most they are catechumens, they are certainly not members. The Didache (c.110 A.D.) says 'But let no one eat or drink of your eucharist but those who have baptized in the name of the Lord. For about this also the Lord has said "Do not give what is holy to the dogs".' (R. C. D. Jasper and G. J. Cuming (eds.) *Prayers of the Eucharist* I *Early and Reformed* (Collins, 1975) p.15). We do not have to adapt the dominical saying to this use, but can still agree that this is the proper discipline.

At St. John's College we once had an unbaptized Jew who was in exactly this situation—as he was hesitant to be baptized until there were more understanding of his conversion on the part of his family. The question was, could such a man, whose faith was orthodox and undoubted, be admitted to communion in College? There was some friendly disagreement within College about this, but the traditional discipline prevailed. He became most obviously a catechumen. But in due course he was baptized—being moved in that direction all the more strongly through our refusal to anticipate baptism.

In sum, there is nothing one *can* offer to unbaptized believers except baptism. It is to baptism, and to baptism pre-eminently, that their attention must be drawn. There is no other way of accepting them into membership or fellowship.

3. PASTORAL PROBLEMS

Baptism usually arises as a matter of discussion or dispute when some practical question is in the offing. It has been the purpose of these Grove Booklets to handle the practical and pastoral questions, and it may be useful now to do a round-up of the most pressing questions, with an examination of the light thrown upon them by the positions I have tried to establish in the last two chapters. The first two problems mentioned below are handled more in earlier booklets than in this one, but the doctrinal arguments hang together in such a way that cross-referencing is possible.

1 Is there a case for infant baptism?

There is of course *A Case for Infant Baptism* (booklet no. 20), but it may still be argued that the *'Case'* is not a 'case'. The case in the *Case* is strengthened by the arguments above that there is no way of treating anyone as Christian except by baptizing him.[1] Christian parents have no way of bringing up their children as believers on this basis except by baptizing them at the outset. This coinheres with the argument in the *Case* that there *is* 'faith' in a newborn infant[2]; that the Old Testament covenant and circumcision point to the baptism of infants of Christian parents[3]; and, of course, that the baptism of households in the New Testament points the same way.[4] In addition, the counter-argument that baptism is no baptism without conscious faith is undercut by the argument here on page 11 above. Even if the infant has no conscious faith, an objectively given baptism *is still a baptism*. That does not amount to a commendation of baptism for infants, but it does open the possibility of it.

2 Which infants should be baptized?

This is the theme of booklet no. 3, *Baptismal Discipline* and of no. 98, *Policies for Infant Baptism* (1987). There the propriety of baptism for the children of Christian parents is taken for granted, and some guidelines are explored for sorting out which parents are entitled to be treated as Christian. The arguments here only touch on that question insofar as baptism is (in a transitional period, in an imperfect world, and with a fallible church) still administered to many infants who perhaps ought not to be viewed as qualified to receive it. The implication of the arguments above is that not only is an infant baptism a true baptism, to be recognized as such, but that this is still the case for an infant baptism which (it is later claimed) ought never to have been administered at all.[5] Even that regrettable baptism was, and is, a baptism, and cannot be discarded because of any alleged inappropriateness about it at the time it was given.

---

1 See booklet no. 20, p.26-27.
2 Booklet no. 20, p.27 footnote 1.
3 Booklet no. 20, pp.9-12.
4 Booklet no. 20, pp.20-21.
5 It is no part of the present argument to say that all the infant baptisms which *have* been administered *should* have been administered; nor is it being asserted that those who received baptism as infants, when with hindsight it would appear better that they should not have had it administered then, are bound now to be glad that they were baptized. Obviously they can regret it. But *it did happen*. Regretting is not denying. And once the baptism is not denied, then a positive value can be set upon it (as in the Bible) alongside of the regrets. See **pp. 20-21 below**.

3. How do we handle requests for a second baptism?

There have always been, since the Reformation, those who maintained that infant baptism is no baptism, and that therefore older believers should seek 'believer's baptism'. Less frequently, the subjective definition of baptism which underlies this teaching has led those who had been baptized for the first time *as adults* to seek a second baptism—on the grounds that they had not been truly converted when they were first baptized, so that it was therefore not a true baptism.[1] For our present purposes, it does not make much difference which case of a request for 'rebaptism' is in view— the issue remains the same. And, for the first time, the issue now comes home in the Anglican Churches because Anglicans are seeking a 'rebaptism' and are *being encouraged by the clergy to remain Anglicans and still be 'rebaptized'*—indeed a few of the clergy are themselves prepared to administer this washing, whilst many more will connive at it.

The word 'rebaptism' and its cognates are put in inverted commas above and hereafter, because it is usually recognized on both sides of the fence that 'rebaptism' is a meaningless word in the strict sense (just like 'second baptism' in the heading to this section). Most Christians are in fact persuaded that a person can by definition only be baptized once—and the discussion is in the strict sense *not* about whether anyone can be rebaptized, but rather about whether some particular event in a person's life was or was not a baptism at all—and thus whether or not he later is still in need of baptism or not. That is why the discussion in this booklet started with trying to define what sort of an event should rank as a baptism, and what should not.

There is sometimes (but much less commonly) an untheological acceptance of the principle of giving the same person two baptisms—usually on the grounds that if he wants it, it will probably do him good to have it! But this not only transmutes baptism into simply an experience (to be sought and then sought again whenever that particular experience seems desirable), but it also means that the Christians who take responsibility for giving the second 'baptism' to the candidate are themselves aligning the church with the candidate's views. In other words, a second baptism, which is acknowledged to be a second baptism, is like a clock which strikes thirteen. It not only confuses at the time, but, more importantly, it casts doubt upon all other teaching at other times from the same source. Baptism is an *initiatory* sacrament. Repeating initiations does *not* reinforce them—it completely disembowels them. Thus we can *just* imagine a situation where a marriage service is declared null and void (as, e.g., on grounds of lack of banns, or false declarations by the parties, or some technicality). In that case, if the couple were to marry, they would then have to marry at some later point *for the first time*. Services which inaugurate or initiate can only be given 'for the first time'. But suppose a couple were to say 'Yes, we did get married, and we are married, but we want to get married again.' What the church would have to do would not be to arrange a marriage, or connive at such a performance. If it did so, it would not only perform a meaningless ceremony at the time—it would also cast great doubt upon its seriousness at all other times when it performs marriages. No, all the church can do is sit down and labour with the

[1] This is set out in a slightly fuller way in booklet no. 20, pp.28-29.

couple to get them to understand that an initiation ceremony is *by definition* unrepeatable. If some later experience is required, then it can only be by invoking the meaning of original initiation and by conscious reference to it. Thus a couple can reaffirm their marriage vows (and the 're-' refers them back to the original marriage), but they *cannot* 'take' each in marriage as though they had come as bachelor and spinster to *begin* their marriage. There is no way their desire for a marriage *tout simple* can be met, and the church cannot pretend it can be. Talking the matter through, or finding some variant on simple marriage, probably some reaffirmation which depends upon the existence of the original marriage, are the only options open to the church.

The same is true of any other inaugural or opening ceremonies—be they civil or sacred. If a new hydro-electric power-station is being opened by, say, Prince Philip, then an opening ceremony is fixed well in advance to suit the royal diary, at the date when the building is expected to be completed. Sometimes not all goes well. Weather or strikes or unforeseen snags occur and the plant is not quite ready when the royal visitor is due. Nevertheless the opening ceremony is held. The uncompleted work is concealed behind hastily rigged barriers, the place is formally locked up, the helicopter lands the prince where he can walk along a red carpet, meet the management, unlock the door, cut a tape, and press a switch. At this point a little man with a bucket pours some water down the turbine (because the plant is not yet ready for the normal flow) so that when the switch is pressed a light-bulb glows, and the prince can safely declare the power-station open. Of course, once this is all over, they cease the pretence, get down to business, and finish the job in earnest. Then the power starts to flow. But what they do *not* do is have another royal visit to open it a second time. The very nature of an opening ceremony is that it only happens once, even if, as in the cartoon picture here, it actually happens that once at the wrong time. To repeat it is to cast doubt upon the whole ritual words 'I declare this plant open', and thus to pull the rug from under *all* opening ceremonies. The logic of this process is either to multiply opening ceremonies infinitely (on the grounds that, although they are meaningless, it is an interesting experience having the prince to lunch afterwards), or alternatively to despair of the usefulness of them altogether. When a 'once and once only' ceremony is thus vitiated, it can turn into a 'twice or more' ceremony, or into a 'not at all' ceremony. Both tendencies are visible simultaneously in the church to-day in respect of baptism and both are equally destructive of its biblical role.

But although this untheological desire to repeat opening ceremonies for the sake of the experience is to be found, the more normal rationale of a 'rebaptism' is that in fact the first administration was not a baptism at all, and thus it is baptism *ab initio* which is now to be given. And we are then thrown back upon the question of definition— was a given previous event a baptism or not?

The desire for 'rebaptism' usually arises in those who were initially baptized as infants, and perhaps have not been brought up as believers but instead have had an adult conversion. Where the church is convinced that an infant baptism *is* a baptism, then it can no more concede the desire for a second 'opening ceremony' than it can give a second marriage to the same couple, as outlined above. The Church of England accepts the propriety—and thus the validity—of baptizing infants. And thus it cannot accept for a 'rebaptism' anyone who has had an infant baptism which conforms to the wide definition on page 11 above.

What then are we to do with such candidates for 'rebaptism'? The only answer is that we must sit down and labour with their understanding of baptism, till they either accept that they *are* already baptized, or, to our regret (but the option is certainly open to them), take their candidature for 'rebaptism' elsewhere. What we cannot do is to give them the straight baptism they apparently seek. To do so would not only mislead at the time, it would also cast doubt upon *every* infant baptism we administer. We are not just to meet the desire of particular persons for a particular experience—we are engaged in a much wider campaign to get the whole church to understand baptism and to use it aright. So we cannot meet the persons' desires direct, though we may of course be able to offer a renewal of baptismal vows in water.[1]

What then is to be said about infant baptism to these persons? We are not now on quite the same ground as when we are trying to persuade hesitant parents to bring their own offspring to baptism. Then, we have to argue that for Christian parents it is *better* to have their children baptized than not. In the present case, we merely have to establish that, misguided though certain parents may have been twenty, thirty, or forty, years ago when they presented their infants for baptism, and misguided though the church may have been to accept them for baptism, yet, granted these possibilities, even so those infant baptisms *were* baptisms. Those who were thus baptized were, and so still are, baptized persons. They cannot now be candidates for baptism. The discussion should include these factors:

(i) An infant baptism is not to be rejected solely because it was done by pouring and not by submersion.[2]

(ii) An infant baptism is not to be rejected solely on the grounds that the recipient was too young to respond for himself. That would be to say that the church cannot treat infants as children of God until they can respond. That in turn would be to create a wholly artificial 'age of response' (at two years old?) when a response would be treated as credible, though in fact it would presumably be a wholly coached response learned by rote from parents, and of no greater significance than a proxy response by a parent prior to that age.

(iii) An infant baptism is not to be rejected on the grounds that in fact children must be much older even than two or three years old before they can *really* believe. This is erroneous in two ways. Firstly, it is unfair to the faith of young children. The expectation in infant baptism is that children will be brought up *as believers,* and will never know a period of unbelief prior to belief.[3] Secondly, the rejection

1 See Appendix 4 on p.25 below.
2 See Appendix 1 on p.24 below.
3 For an attempt to penetrate the experience of this, see booklet no. 20, page 29, footnote 1. We have to recall all the time that a child, even when of an age to communicate verbally, is only communicating what he has learned to say. He is no more an independent child for being able to articulate. In fact he is to be treated as a dependent child throughout his childhood.

would be wrong even if the argument about the age of belief were to be accepted (which it is not). For we have seen that an opening ceremony, an initiation, a baptism, is still valid even if it preceded the experience of that which it purports to inaugurate.

(iv) An infant baptism is not to be rejected on the grounds that the parents who brought the child for baptism were not believing at the time. Parental faith is extremely important when the church is considering which infants should be admitted to baptism. But once the decision to baptize a particular infant has been made, then the validity of the particular baptism cannot be suspended upon the internal question of whether either or both parents truly believed. The acceptance of a particular infant for baptism may appear, with the benefit of hindsight, to have been a great pity. But he *was* accepted, and he *was* baptized, and it *was* baptism which he then received.

(v) An infant baptism is not to be rejected on the grounds that, although some infants do grow as believers from the start, yet in some particular case this was not so, so that particular baptism is not to be reckoned a baptism. But we have seen that if an adult went through baptism but was not visibly converted, that would still be a baptism.[1] The same argument applies to an infant baptism.

(vi) An infant baptism is not to be rejected on the grounds that the recipient cannot later remember it. It is not important to the fact of being a baptized person that one should remember the baptism. Otherwise even those who have been baptized as adults who later suffered from amnesia, or became geriatric cases, or became simply confused, would presumably thereby cease to be baptized persons at all. And this is absurd. The truth is that the New Testament constantly appeals to the fact of being a baptized person here and now, and not to the memory of what the experience of baptism was like.

(vii) An infant baptism is not to be rejected on the grounds that the recipient did not understand its meaning at the time. It may be allowed that infants presumably do not have an understanding of what is intended and expressed at their baptisms, but adult baptisms too are beset with inadequate information, inadequate commitment, misconceptions, and simply wandering thoughts. The lack of understanding will be all the greater where baptism is administered at the time of professing conversion—as, for instance, with the Philippian jailer and his household (who were Gentiles and had no Jewish background even) during the night of the earthquake, when apparently they had had virtually no instruction whatsoever. Certainly the validity or otherwise of a baptism cannot be suspended upon the fulness or accuracy of the candidate's understanding of it. If it were so, none of us would ever be sure he had actually been baptized.[2]

1 The biblical evidence is set out on pp.7 and 10 above.
2 The point about it being improper to insist upon the full understanding and comprehension of the candidate is important not only because to make the insistence might well invalidate most adult baptisms retrospectively, and not only because it would certainly exclude infant baptism altogether, but also because it has very serious implications for the inclusion of the simple, the backward, and half-witted in the church of God, and might also imperil the certainty of the baptism of the few who did have full understanding if they later lost their memories or turned senile.

We thus conclude that infant baptism must be tested for validity against the definition as we set it out on page 11 above, just as adult baptism must. A baptism is a baptism is a baptism. It must be objectively defined, and be subject to external observation. It must be open to being recorded in a register and on a certificate—and not in pencil or invisible ink. When it has happened, it becomes as much a part of the person as circumcision did for the Old Testament Jews. It can no more be eliminated from the record, or pronounced invalid, than could that so-permanent Jewish archetype of Christian baptism. It is much less exciting, and often even frustrating, to accept that baptism has already happened in one's life, and that therefore there is no opportunity to undergo it now. But the church dare not waver from its firm position as to what a baptism is. It is then up to the individual to gain the maximum possible from knowing he is a baptized person, at whatever apparent loss in not going through an exciting experience.

4. How do we handle people who have already had a 'second baptism'?

I write from a context where such cases occur at intervals. Men come for confirmation, even for ordination, having been twice through the waters, and with the conviction that the second time was the *real* time! This obviously has to be handled sensitively. But the issue is exactly the same as the one above. If an individual is allowed unilaterally to invalidate his own first baptism (usually an infant baptism), then the church is conniving at the undoing of its own sacramental practice and is distorting its beliefs.

If it is necessary (as under question 3 above) to dissuade anyone who is looking for a 'rebaptism', then it is equally necessary to bring to repentance anyone who has actually received it. He cannot be allowed in a pedobaptist denomination to regard his second time in the water as his baptism. He cannot be allowed to shred his first certificate of baptism, and set up a later one as true. Again, the church has to labour to bring him to a right understanding of the situation. I would urge that this right understanding would be best expressed by the drawing up of renunciation of the second event. He can then sign it in the presence of witnesses, include it in the baptismal register of his local church, and perhaps even send a copy to the congregation where he was 'rebaptized'. Such a form might read as follows:

'I,.., having received Christian baptism at .... on ....(day .... (month) .... (year), was subsequently 'rebaptized' at... on .... (day) .... (month) .... (year). I now renounce any belief that this 'rebaptism' was in fact my Christian baptism, and I revert to my original baptism as my true Christian baptism.

Signed ....
Name in block capitals...
Address ....

....
Witnessed by..
Address ....

....
Date..
Attached to baptismal register of .... church

This approach looks fairly 'tough', but it is not as 'tough' as the approach that would denounce infant baptism as no baptism and urge a second baptism upon those already baptized. The approach here is no more than a defensive move to undergird 'one baptism once'.

5. How do we preach to the baptized?

This is a large question which can only be opened up briefly here. We have to steer between the Scylla of assuring congregations that all is well because they have been baptized, and the Charybdis of denouncing the baptized on the grounds that their baptism will have deceived them into thinking all is well! It looks as though the Pauline method was to use the fact of his hearers' having been baptized to gain leverage to procure their growth. In effect he said 'You have been baptized into Jesus as Lord—now live for Jesus as your Lord'. It will be seen that this sort of approach neither offers false assurance, nor unnecessarily denounces baptism. It treats it positively, as the starting-point of the Christian life, and as the permanent reminder to the believer of what that Christian life implies.

The evangelical has probably most to learn from this. Our practice of infant baptism has been insufficiently undergirded by doctrinal reasoning so that we have not known how to preach it. Infant baptism, once administered, has been allowed to drop out of sight, instead of providing the framework and the incentive to Christian living. There is considerable recovery of lost ground needed here.

This is particularly true in 'evangelistic' preaching. Baptism is the one feature of the Christian life—the initial feature—which the hearers may have. Thus evangelism has a foothold in the life of the hearers, as one feature of the gospel has already been received.[1] This must not be ignored, but utilized. If of course the hearers have never been baptized, then that is the truest evangelism of all. In such cases the evangel must include the call to baptism, and submission to the evangel must be effected in baptism. That is the New Testament way.[2]

[1] The point here is that the preacher should rarely be saying 'You have been baptized, and much good it has done you!' The better emphasis is surely to be able to say 'You have been baptized into Jesus as Lord. Let him be your Lord.' If the nature of the faith-relationship with Jesus Christ, the incorporation into his body the church, and his expectations and call to a life of holiness, are all built upon the meaning of baptism (and they are all there in the New Testament passages on baptism), then not only is the leverage of the word most operative (because it is treating the fulcrum of baptism as secure), but also any who are converted this way will not be denouncing their baptism as having misled them, but rather rejoicing that it has now come to fruition. This approach does of course mean that the preacher does not separate between sheep and goats as he preaches to the congregation, and if goats become sheep they do so in relatively unspectacular ways as the truth of God gradually takes over in their lives without them necessarily noticing when. To denounce their past is to ask for a crisis conversion—to build on it is to accept a slow one.

[2] The logical implication of this is that when a man wishes to come to faith, the first question to be asked him is 'Are you baptized or not?'. If he is, then he is formally apostate and needs to be restored, and his existing baptism must be handled positively (as shown above), and not derogatorily. But if he is not baptized, then he must be shown baptism as the point of commitment and surrender, and must be offered the chance to have it whenever he wishes to be converted. He will also need to be shown that he can take his children into baptism with him . . .

APPENDIXES

1 THE MODE OF BAPTISM

In booklet no. 20 I argued on page 31 that pouring or affusion is sufficient for a baptism to be a baptism. I should perhaps add, over against those who insist on submersion, that the symbolism of death and resurrection is no more foundational in the New Testament than that of new birth or incorporation or 'putting on Christ' or even washing. Even if it were foundational, it would *still* leave the mode an open question. Christians need to get clear in their minds that biblical symbolism is not to be identified with dramatic enactment, even though there may be some points of resemblance between the symbol and that which it symbolizes. Thus the Lord's Supper cannot contain any *dramatization* of Calvary. The symbolism derives from Jesus' attachment of meaning to particular elements and actions, and *not* from any ability of ours to do these actions in such a way as to suggest verisimilitude. So it is with baptism. Submersion may be appropriate and powerful, but it cannot be requisite. David Pawson conceded this point in booklet no. 24 page 18.

2 THE 'FORMULA' OF BAPTISM

There is sometimes encountered a sterile little argument about whether candidates ought to be baptized 'in the name of the Father and the Son and the Holy Spirit' (Matt. 28.19) or 'in the name of the Lord Jesus' (Acts 2.38, 10.48 etc.). I have even met a case where the slightly more ecstatic fringe of Christian believers baptized a girl in the sea with one formula, brought her out, questioned their own use of that formula, took her back in and did her again with the other one! When we recall that at the time of Hippolytus in the West there was neither formula in use, it may be that this is a woodenly superficial quest. Surely the New Testament phrases refer to the meaning of baptism, and *not* to the text used at the administration? Thus Paul can say the Corinthians were 'baptized into Moses' (1 Cor. 10.1), not implying anything about a formula, but only about the meaning (of being committed to Moses' headship.) On this score the Matthean phrases and the Lukan ones in the Acts of the Apostles do not conflict at all—both forms of words express briefly the significance of baptism, and, as neither does it exhaustively in just a handful of words, it is not surprising that they both differ from each other, yet cohere perfectly. So no question of formula is to be shipped into the definition on page 10 above.

3 THE MINISTER OF BAPTISM

According to traditional 'Catholic' theology, any person, ordained or lay, male or female, may in necessity give baptism. Indeed, even heretics may give valid baptism on this view. There has been a 'puritan' view around which tied the authority to give baptism tightly to the authority to minister the word of God. But this was a disciplinary concept, which would only be used by the most rigorist thinkers as a basis for invalidating baptisms done by lay-people. In general, the insistence that there is but 'one baptism' in common to all believers ought to leave us expecting to recognize as a baptism anything which claims to be (even if conducted without a congregation in a home, or within an unusual denomination or *ad hoc* gathering), unless there is evidence that the person had been previously baptized, or that the context was demonstrably non-Christian.

4. RENEWAL OF BAPTISMAL VOWS IN WATER

Since the second edition of the Booklet was published in 1983 I have become more and more sympathetic to the provision of a rite for renewing baptismal vows *in water,* and have practised this when in Birmingham diocese.

The starting point of the discussion of any such provision must be that infant baptism once given *is* baptism, and the person who received it *cannot* now be baptized.[1] But at the same time, the desire for the swamping of submersion, and for the subjective sense of totality in God's grace and in his or her own commitment—that desire can, I judge, be met without compromising the once-for-allness of the baptism already given. Indeed I compare such provision to the provision we already make for the candidate to articulate the baptismal vows with his or her own mouth. Such articulation properly belongs with the baptism itself, but at an infant baptism it is made by proxy. The candidate, when of age to answer in his or her own person, then adds that personal profession—whether at confirmation or any other similar event. If the original baptism can stand, even if it lacks something which is appropriate (though not, on our definitions, absolutely necessary), so, by parity of argument, a case can be made for adding at a later age the subjective experience of a swamping submersion.

The important point is that, even if conducted at a baptismal event, it must not be open either at the time or later to being interpreted as being initiatory baptism.[2] Thus I suggest five fences to be put round such an event to defend it against any misunderstanding or misinterpretation:[2]

1. In *preparation* the candidate must acknowledge that he is already a baptized person.

2. In public *profession,* whether at the time of the event or at a service prior to it, the candidate must acknowledge this before the baptism takes place.

3. In the *preaching* of the sermon the preacher should distinguish very carefully between baptism and renewal of baptismal vows.

4. In the *liturgical* use, every reference to the event must make it clear that the candidate comes to the water already baptized.[4]

5. In the *registration* of the event, certification of what occurred should be put into the candidate's hands, into the baptismal register (by fixing a looseleaf account in for the right date by paperclip, not by adding new entries of baptism), into the service register, and into any parish magazine.

[1] See pp.18-21 above.
[2] In Autumn 1987 the House of Bishops of the Church of England passed resolutions which cautioned about the use of any non-baptismal rite which could be mistaken for baptism. I, of course, agree entirely.
[3] I have written this up slightly more fully in my chapter in Donald Withey (ed.) *Adult Initiation* (Alcuin/GROW Joint Liturgical Study no. 10, 1989) pp.32-33.
[4] At the submersion the text I have come to use runs as follows: 'N. as you have been baptized into the name of the Father and of the Son and of the Holy Spirit, so now in commemoration of that baptism and in renewal of its meaning to you I dip you in this water in the name of the Father and of the Son and of the Holy Spirit.'

STOCK LIST—GROVE BOOKLETS ON MINISTRY & WORSHIP [Nos. 1-70]
and **GROVE WORSHIP SERIES** [71 onwards]

The Worship Series (of 24 pages each) is now published four times a year. All titles cost **£1.40** in 1990.
Numbers not included below are out of print. Asterisked titles are in a second edition or reprint.

*12. **The Language of Series 3** by David L. Frost
*14. **Recent Liturgical Revision in the Church of England** by Colin Buchanan (**£2.50**)†
14A. **Supplement for 1973-4 to Recent Liturgical Revision in the Church of England** by Colin Buchanan
14B. **Supplement for 1974-6 to Recent Liturgical Revision in the Church of England** by Colin Buchanan
14C. **Supplement for 1976-8 to Recent Liturgical Revision in the Church of England** by Colin Buchanan
14D. See Liturgical Study 39 (**£2.50**)†
15. **Institutions and Inductions** by Trevor Lloyd
16. **Alternative Eucharistic Prayers** by Derek Billings
*20. **A Case for Infant Baptism** by Colin Buchanan
*24. **Infant Baptism under Cross-Examination** by David Pawson and Colin Buchanan
29. **The Ordinal and its Revision** by Peter Toon
30. **Liturgy and Creation** by Peter R. Akehurst
32. **Inaugural Services** Edited by Colin Buchanan
*35. **Drama in Worship** by Andy Kelso
40. **Freedom in a Framework: Some Possibilities with Series 3** by Richard More
*42. **Christian Healing in the Parish** by Michael Botting
43. **Modern Roman Catholic Worship: Baptism and Penance** by Nicholas Sagovsky
*44. **Exorcism, Deliverance and Healing: Some Pastoral Guidelines** by John Richards
50. **Evangelicals, Obedience and Change** by Trevor Lloyd
52. **Inter-Faith Worship?** by Peter Akehurst and Dick Wootton
53. **Penance** by David Gregg
*55. **Urban Church Growth: Some Clues from Britain and South America** by Eddie Gibbs
60. **Liturgy for Ordination: The Series 3 Services** by Michael Sansom
*61. **One Baptism Once** by Colin Buchanan
*62. **Preaching at Funerals** by Colin Buchanan
65. **Liturgy for Initiation: The Series 3 Services** by Colin Buchanan
66. **Encountering Westindian Pentecostalism: its Ministry and Worship** by John Root
68. **Liturgy for Communion: The Revised Series 3 Service** by Colin Buchanan
*70. **Preaching at Baptisms** by Gordon Ogilvie
71. **A Hymn Book Survey 1962-1980** by Robin A. Leaver
72. **A Late-Night Service: Compline in Modern English** by Mark Davies
73. **Family Festivals: An Approach to Worship in the Home** compiled by Michael Vasey, Tom Jamieson, Lyn Jamieson, Dan Young and Sue Young
*74. **Preaching at Weddings** by Ian Bunting
75. **Ceremonial in Worship** by Trevor Lloyd
*76. **Leading Worship** by Colin Buchanan
*77. **Intercessions in Worship** by Michael Vasey
78. **Preaching at Communion (i)** by Ian Bunting
79. **Preaching at Communion (ii)** by Ian Bunting
80. **The Kiss of Peace** by Colin Buchanan
81. **Hymns in Today's Language?** by Chris Idle
82. **Eucharistic Concelebration** by John Fenwick
83. **Renewing the Congregation's Music** by David Parkes
84. **Liturgy for the Sick: The New Church of England Services** by Colin Buchanan and David Wheaton
85. **Welcoming Children to Communion** by Dan Young
87. **Introducing Liturgical Change** by Trevor Lloyd
88. **Welcoming the Bishop** by David Cutts
89. **Preaching on Special Occasions** by Charles Hutchins
90. **Evangelical Anglicans and Liturgy** by Colin Buchanan
91. **Adult Baptisms** by Colin Buchanan
92. **Evangelical Anglicans and the Lima Text** by Tony Price
93. **Celebrating Lent Holy Week and Easter** by Trevor Lloyd
94. **Reading the Bible at the Eucharist** by Michael Vasey
95. **Worship in the Inner City** by John Bentham
96. **Extended Communion—an Experiment in Cumbria** by David Smethurst
97. **Celebrating The Agape Today** by Trevor Lloyd
98. **Policies for Infant Baptism** by Colin Buchanan
99. **Remembrance Sunday** by Andrew K. Jones
100. **The Future of Anglican Worship** compiled by Trevor Lloyd, on behalf of The Group for Renewal of Worship (GROW)
101. **Anglicans and Worship in Local Ecumenical Projects** by Colin Buchanan
102. **Initiating Adults: Lessons from The Roman Catholic Rite** by Paul Tudge
103. **Contemporary Eucharistic Prayers** by David Kennedy and David Mann
104. **The Laying on of Hands in The Parish Healing Ministry** by Carolyn Headley
105. **The Eucharist with Congregational Action** by Maggie Durran
106. **Lambeth and Liturgy 1988** edited by Colin Buchanan
107. **Revising The ASB** by Colin Buchanan
108. **Worship in Small Congregations** by David Cutts
109. **Sunday Evening Worship** by David Kennedy and David Mann
110. **Worship in the Restoration Movement** by James Steven

†14, 14A, 14B, 14C, Liturgical Study 39 available together for **£7.50**

ISSN 0305-3067   **ISBN** 1 85174 126 7

GROVE BOOKS LIMITED

BRAMCOTE   NOTTS.   NG9 3DS (0602-430786)

Printed by Hassall & Lucking Ltd., Cross Street, Long Eaton, Nottingham NG10 1HD   Tel. L.E. 733292